UNFORGETTABLE

YOUR PURPOSE IN CHRIST
REVISED & UPDATED

MATT SWEETMAN

MCA THE CHURCH
MORENO VALLEY

13830 Nason St
Moreno Valley, CA 92555

MCATHECHURCH.COM

Significant Read

Chicago, Illinois

Unforgettable - Your Purpose in Christ
Revised & updated

Matt Sweetman
P.O. BOX 1492, Chicago, IL 60690-1492 USA
SignificantRead.com
connect@SignificantRead.com

Edited by James Priest

ISBN-13: 978-0615694009

DEDICATION

I'd like to dedicate this book to my wife and children.

Heather, you are the most unforgettable person I have ever met. You are beautiful, genuine, and too much fun. I love you babe. Let's count each day we have, always doing our best to remember who we are in Christ.

Jones, Macrae, Paisley, and Finley, you are uniquely unforgettable. I love you guys so much. I hope that we get to make some of the best memories of our lives together. I pray that as you grow, you will continue to find your identity and purpose in Christ alone.

CONTENTS

WHY READ THIS BOOK?

Hopefully you received this book because you were a guest at church. If you desire to give this book to others, I'd like to ask that instead of sharing it or buying a copy, please encourage them to pick up their own copy like you did. What I say will make more sense after visiting church.

Visiting a church is a significant thing to do, and so this book is intended to help you make the most of your experience, whether you are a believer or not. But more than that, its goal is to invest in you and help you make sense of your whole life. I want to say a huge thank you for going to church. It's so important to be with Jesus and His people. But you can't just leave it at that. It's critical that you make your experience more meaningful.

I want to ask you to read this book because you can't afford to miss its central point. Most people have not figured out why they exist. Some have confident assertions, but underneath there is often a nagging sense of uncertainty. This book can help you think about the purpose of your life in a meaningful way.

I also want to ask you to read this book to honor those who spent the time and money to purchase it for you. The greatest thing to do with a gift is to use it.

If you are still hesitant to give this book a try, why not just commit to read the first chapter? I honestly think you'll find it helpful.

Are you ready to discover an unforgettable purpose?

1

COMEBACK

There is no remembrance of former things, nor will there be any remembrance of later things yet to be among those who come after.
- Ecclesiastes 1:11

The author of the book of Ecclesiastes has a timeless and sobering message: eventually the world will forget us. Maybe we think our efforts and contributions will benefit future generations, but as the universe decays and eventually all energy is scattered beyond our use (as science predicts), every contribution we've ever made to humanity will be annihilated and therefore forgotten. This saddening conclusion begs the question: if no one will be around to remember and benefit from our efforts, does anything matter?

I understand that starting a book on such a low emotional point may not seem like the best idea. Nevertheless, we must either conclude that this dreadful problem has a solution, or we must conclude that our life will mean nothing. If you have categorically decided that life is meaningless, stop reading. If you are still reading, this book will reveal the solution to be quite unforgettable. Bear with me here: things will get darker before they get brighter.

SIGNIFICANCE

If something is unknown, it has no apparent value. If metals of greater worth than gold or platinum exist, it doesn't matter because no human being has ever discovered them. When people are unknown, they lack worth. Who will even think to include them or help them? They cannot be made a priority, elevated in significance, protected or even considered. People feel worthwhile when others assign worth to them.

Even the creation of self-value through weight loss, exercise, fashion, cosmetics, education or any type of "self-improvement" focuses on being significant in the eyes of others. Without other people watching, there is no such thing as noticeable improvement. In the end, our validation comes from an external source.

We all want to feel as though we matter to others, and it stings when people act as though we don't. Have you ever been forgotten? Have you been ignored, excluded, overlooked, or taken for granted? If we didn't care about other people knowing and remembering us, we wouldn't care about being forgotten. Whether intentional or not, we are bothered when the restaurant forgets our order or a loved one forgets a special occasion. When people forget us, it hurts.

Have you ever considered why the most important person in your life matters so much to you? Perhaps they care about you more than anyone else. Maybe when everyone else might have devalued you, they didn't. Our deepest joys in life come about because other people remember us, and our darkest moments in life come about when people forget us, or remember us incorrectly. To be remembered is to be significant.

LOST MEMORIES

The connection of memory and significance makes it especially painful when our loved ones have memory disorders; a disease erasing a lifetime of shared experience seems unbearable. Death would seem easier to deal with, until we remember that death ultimately terminates a person's unique memories, which in turn means the loss in value of all they cared about as a person. Unless carefully recorded, all that the mind had uniquely experienced and deemed valuable is gone.

If everyone who values you dies, no one really knows you anymore. You are not just alone; you become insignificant. Then when *you* die, most (if not all) of your life will be forgotten after only two generations. Somebody would have to cheat death in order to perpetuate the true significance of their life from one generation to another, but who can do that?

UNKNOWN MOMENTS

Most things in our lives will remain unknown. In my early twenties I sat in the basement of an enormous and frustratingly out-of-date paper filing system as I considered my life and the job I despised. Time stood still for a moment as I contemplated my present situation and its insignificance. I wondered if that mundane moment had any meaning whatsoever. I have many more situations in my life—as do you—that are unknown, and will forever remain that way. Are they, therefore, meaningless?

I once met a construction worker whose glasses fell into his cement mixer as he poured it into the foundation of a major road in Kansas City. Thousands of people drive over his glasses every day with no knowledge of their presence beneath the surface of the road. How many countless moments of human existence will remain unknown? Who could even have a mind to retain them all?

People try to circumvent this dilemma by writing books, making movies, building statues, or naming something after themselves. Not everyone has the opportunity or aptitude to achieve this, and even when they do, we don't really know them. Learning the facts of history and reading biographies can be rewarding, but even the best historians can only report what they remember from their research. The world forgets countless people every day; who can keep track of them all?

HISTORY REPEATING

What has been is what will be, and what has been done is what will be done, and there is nothing new under the sun. **- Ecclesiastes 1:9**

After countless generations of war, violence and oppression, humanity still struggles with them. Some generations who survive war take stock in the loss of life and think it unimaginable that the world would tolerate such horrors again. Because future generations don't share those terrible experiences, however, those events begin to lose significance and history repeats. On the other hand, some will not let history go. They fiercely hold onto generational offenses and repeat the same horrors. Either way this truth is the same; what's remembered becomes important and what's forgotten is not.

Some people pretend they don't want to be remembered. Some think lowly of themselves and dislike attention, but any hint of selfishness shows we value ourselves above others. Deep down we all crave some level of attention. We are all searching for significance. We want to be significant to someone, whether it's a family member, romantic interest, co-worker, company, group, school, friend, the person next door, or even a pet.

DOES ANYTHING MATTER?

What does man gain by all the toil at which he toils under the sun? A generation goes, and a generation comes, but the earth remains forever. **- Ecclesiastes 1:3-4**

Every generation thinks they are significant, but when they die, the world keeps spinning just the same without them. Much of life's work will be eventually undone, no matter the profession. Every person whom a doctor cures becomes sick again and eventually dies. Our buildings crumble. Our money is spent, lost or stolen. Our companies close their doors. Our innovations become obsolete. Our mighty nations and empires collapse. Unfortunately, most of the work we have accomplished today, this week, or this month, will be forgotten. If we cannot guarantee that what we do will have meaning in the future, is everything we do meaningless?

In Ecclesiastes 1:1, the author refers to himself as "the Preacher, the son of David, king in Jerusalem." Historians guess he is King Solomon, but the certainty of his true identity has been forgotten, which illustrates my point. The author says he "applied his heart to seek and to search out by wisdom all that is done under heaven," and at the end of his studies he declared that all life was "vanity," though a more literal translation would read "vapor." In other words, he pursued the avenues of human reasoning and concluded that all of human existence is here one moment and gone the next. Scientists tell us that one day our sun will burn out. Unless we can build technology to escape it or prevent it, that's it, game over: every person and thing, eternally forgotten.

Is there any hope? Should we just try to be happy and reckon our lives to have no transcendent consequence? Is the son of David right in saying that you and I are just vapor? The answer is revealed at the end of the book of Ecclesiastes. If you will just hear the words of the Preacher, the son of David, king in Jerusalem, it will save you a lifetime of searching.

THE SOLUTION

The end of the matter, all has been heard. Fear God and keep his commandments, for this is the whole duty of man. For God will bring every deed into judgment, with every secret thing, whether good or evil. **- Ecclesiastics 12:13-14**

The God of the Bible knows every secret and will bring about real consequences for every deed. He doesn't just know about glasses buried under a highway or mundane jobs, He knows everything unspoken and unknown. Every. Single. Thing. He knows all the things we have forgotten, or that we hope no one else will ever know. It is an awesome thing that God holds all of humanity accountable for their lives. Someone has to bring justice to all the injustice, otherwise the world just doesn't make sense.

Fear, then, is a natural response to the God of the Bible. It's not like the fear of heights, but more like the tension we feel when a police officer pulls us over, or the tax man wants to audit us. They have authority over us and will bring about real consequences in our lives. We naturally try to respect them in these moments. It is infinitely more so with God. We should be in awe of Him because of His authority over us.

GOD REMEMBERS

This distinction separates the God of the Bible from every other system of spirituality: He not only knows about everything we do, He is personally concerned about it. If God purposefully remembers every moment of our life, we can find eternal value in Him. The only good answer to the problem of insignificance is that God knows and cares about what we do with our lives.

Psalm 8:4 records a prayer from King David: "What is man that you are mindful of him, and the son of man that you care for him?" The prophet Isaiah proclaims that even mothers can forget about their babies (which sounds unimaginable, but children are misplaced or abandoned every day), yet God makes this promise to His people: "I will not forget you" (Isaiah 49:15). People are always on God's mind; how wonderful is that?

WHICH GOD?

If God is only a force in the universe without intellect, then true justice is impossible. Someone with supreme reason must determine and deliver real consequences. Without a God who thinks, our lives will be forgotten. If God is not personal, then He can neither relate to us nor hold each one accountable. The Bible tells us that God is even more personal than we could have imagined. Many of us want to think of Jesus merely as a "good teacher", but Jesus claimed to be equal to God Himself (John 5:18). As C.S. Lewis has so famously pointed out, no "good teacher" makes such claims; we must decide if Jesus was lying, crazy, or God.

The description that the author of Ecclesiastes gives himself is mysteriously suited for Jesus, even though it was written hundreds of years before Christ's birth. Jesus is the ultimate preacher (Mark 1:22), the true son of David (Matthew 21:9), and the real king in Jerusalem (John 12:13). In fact, there are over three hundred predictions of Jesus' life long before He was born. Some are so specific they even tell us the amount of money He would be betrayed for: thirty pieces of silver (Zechariah 11:12). Jesus is the author behind the author. His identity may have been previously obscured to you, but He's the person we've all been looking for.

We not only need a God who is all-knowing and who cares, we need a God who cannot die. His memories must stay alive forever, otherwise all our work and every moment in our lives will become meaningless. Most great religious leaders have tombs, except for the most famous one. Jesus is not just one of the most unforgettable historical figures, He is the only one who has ever beaten death. Christians do not gather to His tomb because He doesn't have one. Don't you find it odd that one of the most influential figures in history doesn't have a grave? He has made the most unforgettable comeback in human history.

If Jesus wasn't resurrected, then we have some difficult things to explain. How did the disciples, who abandoned Jesus, manage to convince people He had risen? Why did the Romans not just produce Jesus' body? Why did His disciples not recant when they were tortured to death? Why would they die for a cause that wasn't real? Why would thousands of people suddenly decide to become Christians if there was no proof? The most unforgettable event in history must have more to it than we've previously thought.

The resurrection shows that Jesus has beaten death and that He lives forever. Because He cannot die, He therefore has the only mind that can equally remember and value each person's work, service, activity, relationships, attitudes, and secrets from one generation to the next. Every person who wants to be remembered needs to live only for the approval and acceptance of Jesus. So if every deed, good or evil, will be brought under God's judgment, what will the verdict be for each of us? How do we know if we will measure up?

THE BIG TEN

What God remembers about us, He measures by His standards. That is why the author of Ecclesiastes says to "keep his commandments." Most of us are familiar with the basics of God's Law, otherwise known as the Ten Commandments: no lying, no stealing, no adultery, no murder; you get the idea. But that's not the end of it. Jesus said God considers hatred to be murder and lust to be adultery (Matthew 5:22,28). They aren't just "actions," but "attitudes," hidden to all but God. No human can ever live up to this standard. Because God has an impeccable memory, we are all in trouble.

One person was able to live the perfect life that God requires. Jesus kept the outward and inward requirements of God, yet He was punished as if He had failed them. We generally think that if we do good things, good things will happen to us. Jesus lived an exemplary life, yet died a horrible death, which contradicts our do-good-get-good theory. "For our sake he made him to be sin who knew no sin, so that in him we might become the righteousness of God" (2 Corinthians 5:21). In other words, Jesus switched places with us. He absorbed our sin and judgment. We can now freely receive His righteousness and its consequence—absolute freedom from every wrong action and attitude. Followers of Christ are no longer accountable to the Law (Ephesians 2:14-15). Given that none of us could ever keep the Law in full, what Christ has done is truly the best news anyone could ever hear.

How do we respond to this news? Is it as simple as "trying harder" or "doing good"? No.

In Luke 18, Jesus meets a wealthy ruler. This man believes he is a good person. He didn't understand that God expects more than good behavior. Jesus understood it, though, and so He tests the ruler's attitudes by asking him to give away his wealth to help the poor. The young man, who thought he was a good person, walked away from Jesus because he loved his money more than he loved God. Thus, he broke the first requirement, which is to love God more than anything else (Exodus 20:3-4). Being good to gain a relationship with God is useless because none of us can be good enough. We will always put other things in place of God, and that's not good.

FOLLOWING CHRIST

If you want to follow Christ, you must surrender everything to Him. Every. Single. Thing. Call out to Him from the depths of your soul. Admit that He is the only way to know God. Nothing else, and no one else, can save you. Confess your wrong actions and attitudes to Him and repent of them. Ask His forgiveness. Trust that He switched places for you. Believe that His blood ran down that Roman cross. Believe that He died and rose again three days later. Pledge all the things in your life to be under His discretion. Give and serve. Thank Jesus that He was forgotten by God so you could be eternally remembered and valued. Turn over everything to Jesus.

"For by grace you have been saved through faith. And this is not your own doing; it is the gift of God, not a result of works, so that no one may boast" (Ephesians 2:8-9). The quality of our devotion and the extensiveness of our repentance have nothing to do with receiving salvation, they are simply the response. We come to know God only by His complete initiation and kindness towards us. Let your decision to follow Christ be real and from the heart, but know that only His grace redeems. Place your faith in His grace. Trust in Jesus alone. That's true salvation.

If you want to follow Christ for the first time, or if you are coming back to Him, you must tell people in your life, otherwise you're just giving lip service to God. It's especially important that you tell another Christian so they can help you. The next step for all who decide to follow Jesus is baptism in water. The Apostle Peter told the crowd: "Repent and be baptized *every one of you* in the name of Jesus Christ for the forgiveness of your sins, and you will receive the gift of the Holy Spirit" (Acts 2:38, italics mine).

If you aren't ready to surrender everything to Jesus right now, still pray to Him. Ask that He will reveal Himself to you. Get connected to others who have a relationship with Jesus. Don't let your life be forgettable. For many, the process of salvation can take time, so don't sabotage it. Take one more step in the right direction.

STAGE YOUR COMEBACK

How do you make the most of what you have been reading? You must go back to church at your next opportunity. You might feel uncertain, disconnected, insecure, or that you don't fit in, but at the end of the day, if you have any desire to belong to Jesus, then you belong in Jesus' family. Don't let previous hurt, preconceived ideas or fear stop you from living an unforgettable life. You'll never truly know what a church is like if you don't give it another shot. Other people there may feel just as nervous or uncertain as you are. Extend some grace, like God did for you.

The goal of a life that trusts Jesus is to be like Jesus. In 1 Corinthians 11:1 the Apostle Paul says, "Be imitators of me, as I am of Christ." We imitate Christ by interacting with and copying the Christ-like behavior of other believers. We can't do it alone. We will always become like the people we spend time with. To be like Jesus, we must spend time with people who are being like Jesus.

Jesus is building an eternal and unforgettable community. One of the most impacting ways we can be like Jesus is to love His church. "Husbands, love your wives, as Christ loved the church and gave himself up for her" (Ephesians 5:25). No one loves the church as much as Jesus, so I dare you to imitate His love for the church. Change your plans, rearrange your schedule, adjust your priorities, make a concerted effort to be with Jesus and His people. Make an unforgettable comeback.

If our goal is to be known and remembered by Jesus, how do we go about truly knowing Him? We'll deal with that in chapter two.

My next steps are to ...

☐ Commit to go back to church as soon as possible
☐ Commit my entire life to following Jesus
☐ Commit myself to water baptism
☐ Read chapter 2

2

SITBACK

Now as they went on their way, Jesus entered a village. And a woman named Martha welcomed him into her house. And she had a sister called Mary, who sat at the Lord's feet and listened to his teaching. But Martha was distracted with much serving. And she went up to him and said, "Lord, do you not care that my sister has left me to serve alone? Tell her then to help me." But the Lord answered her, "Martha, Martha, you are anxious and troubled about many things, but one thing is necessary. Mary has chosen the good portion, which will not be taken away from her". - **Luke 10:38-42**

This unforgettable encounter shows us how to experience Jesus. We can know and receive from Jesus today just as His first disciples did. The greatest thing in life is to know Jesus and to hear Him speak grace and truth over us.

Jesus gathered thousands upon thousands to hear His profound and provocative words "...the crowds were *astonished* at his teaching" (Matthew 7:28, italics mine). He captivated hearts so intensely, people followed Him to desolate places without food (Matthew 14:13-15). Even the religious leaders who wanted to kill Him said: "No one ever spoke like this man!" (John 7:46).

Jesus doesn't shroud His teaching in religious nonsense. He doesn't give steps to success or try to sell you something. He speaks plainly, and with real authority. The words themselves seemed to change people. Some of His disciples commented: "Did not our hearts burn within us while he talked?" (John 24:32). Peter even said to Him: "You have the words of eternal life" (John 6:68). If we want to know Jesus, we must listen to Him and discover why His disciples say He is the Word of God (John 1:1).

Mary sat at Jesus' feet and listened. She gave Jesus her undivided attention. Jesus was so pleased with her decision, He affirmed to everyone present that she had chosen the "good portion", and He promised it would not be taken from her. We often think that "being good" means we're doing something, but Jesus says otherwise. He has the authority to define what is good (Matthew 28:18). Jesus valued Mary's intentional inactivity in His presence far more than Martha's busy serving. In other words, Jesus is telling us to sit back and listen.

OUR DILEMMA

When it comes to our goodness and our activity, it's easy for us to get it backward. We tend to feel good about ourselves based on our achievements, but when was the last time you truly felt you'd done enough? Living for the passing thrills of our own success is an endless rat race. If we want genuine fulfillment, we must give up our self-absorbed activity and learn to sit with Jesus.

Psalm 46:10 says: "Be still, and know that I am God". We cannot encounter God if we insist on frantic activity and finger-pointing. Martha had the God of the universe in her living room, in the flesh, but her action-oriented ideology caused her to miss the wonder of it. Jesus is just as present with us as He was with Martha all those years ago. Even in this moment God is inviting each of us to rest in Him. This invitation requires us to stop what we are doing, even good things, in order to meet with Jesus.

In a world that seems stuck in fast forward, the idea of slowing down sounds impossible. Our calendars are filled with social events, appointments, and travel plans; our days are filled with striving. We consume entertainment, apps, sports, and waste hours online. But to what end? Despite the fact that we have more conveniences than at any other time in history, we still claim to have no time.

Our issue is simple, we are anxious and troubled by things that don't matter. They just don't matter. Spending time with Jesus is the last thing many believers prioritize. We need a radical reorientation towards the value and practice of enjoying a friendship with Jesus.

We will always have demands on us, but nothing is more necessary than our need for God. Jesus proclaims: "Come to me, all who are heavy laden, and I will give you rest" (Matthew 11:28). The all-powerful creator of the universe is giving you permission to break from the ridiculously forgettable activities that want to consume your time, to find refreshment in Him, and to receive everything He wants to give to you. Experiencing God's rest is the ultimate purpose of following Christ (Hebrews 4:11) and the key to leading an unforgettable life.

JESUS' MESSAGE

What exactly is Jesus' message? Why is it so different from other religious leaders? The answer is in the crowd's astonishment: "they marveled at the *gracious* words that were coming out of his mouth" (Luke 4:22, italics mine). Jesus illustrates the good news of God's radical kindness by demonstrating grace in its purest, most powerful, and most abundant form (John 1:16). In a world full of self-improvement and maintaining appearances, nothing is more radically different, freeing, and enjoyable than the grace of Jesus. Sure, He was unapologetic about sin and judgment, but that only served to magnify His almost irrational kindness towards sinners.

Jesus spends a lot of time teaching about unconditional grace —people receiving everything for nothing. Grace is like birds who find shelter in trees they didn't plant (Matthew 4:30-32), and crops producing food without our effort (Mark 4:26-29). Grace is like finding a priceless treasure hidden in a field (Matthew 13:44). Jesus' grace delivers justice to the exploited, harmed, or ignored (Luke 10:30-37, 18:2-5), and those who squander family wealth are welcomed back with parties (Matthew 15:11-32). Jesus spreads grace by telling others to speak of all He has done for them (Mark 5:19).

Jesus' grace does not stop with words. He shows grace through His miracles: healing sickness (Matthew 12:15), feeding hungry crowds (Matthew 14:13-21), even raising a widow's son back to life (Luke 7:11-17). He shows grace by saving an adulterous woman from being stoned to death by an angry mob (John 8:3-11), by washing His disciples' feet (John 13:5), and by cooking breakfast for those same disciples after they abandoned Him (John 21:12). Ultimately He shows us grace by allowing Himself to be tortured and executed in order to pay the price of our sin (John 3:16), defeating death by resurrection (Luke 24), and sending us the gift of the Holy Spirit (Acts 2:1-8, Acts 11:15-17). In Jesus' world of grace, wonderful things happen to people who don't deserve it.

GOOD NEWS OF GRACE

The Bible describes the grace of God in this way: "He does not deal with us according to our sins" (Psalm 103:10). Grace means that God extends unconditional acceptance to us, no matter what we have done. Grace means that God illogically forgives, remains committed, and approves of us forever. Grace means that God will never get tired of us, will never exclude us, will never give up on us. Ever. Through His grace, God has made a way for us to experience the kind of loving relationship we've always wanted but never had.

Best of all, grace does not depend on our performance, but on Jesus' perfection, "If the Son sets you free, you will be free indeed" (John 8:36). Jesus has achieved salvation for us, which means our absolute freedom from sin, judgment, and death cannot be revoked. The entire message of the Bible revolves around the unconditional redemption that Jesus offers us, by faith in His grace (Ephesians 2:8). Martha could never know Jesus by doing things for Him, even good things. The good works we do come later, as an outflowing of joy. Mary chose to stop and receive from Jesus first, and Jesus commended her for embracing His grace.

"GETTING" GRACE

The importance of grace is difficult to understand because it forces us to take a hard look at our self-righteousness and recognize that we are much worse off than we thought. Grace means we reject the delusion that living morally can somehow outweigh our failures. Grace means we stop telling ourselves that, despite all of history telling us otherwise, humanity is essentially good and that one day we will manage to get things right. The more we grasp that without Jesus we are selfish, unbelieving sinners drunk on our own opinions, the more God's grace starts to make sense.

If we could just use our imaginations to contemplate an infinitely moral judge, whose mission is to purge the world of evil and establish a perfect community, perhaps we'd get closer to grasping how offensive our sin really is. When we hurt each other, we are working against God's divine plan. All sins then are essentially spiritual crimes against a transcendent and holy God. The ramifications are cosmic. If you lie to your spouse, you might spend the night on the couch. If you lie to your boss, you might lose your job. If you lie under oath, you might go to prison. Same sin, different offenders, and therefore, different levels of consequence.

The consequence of our sin is that it disconnects us from God —the source of life and goodness. Without grace, sin dooms humanity to an eternity of separation. Jesus seems to indicate that hell is a place without remorse (Luke 16:19-26). This depiction of hell may sound tame, or even desirable to some, but hell is far scarier than we imagine—it is the final and unending absence of all that is good.

God does not delight in hell, but is patiently waiting for all people to turn to Him, wanting no one to perish without Him (2 Peter 3:9). He gives all people the opportunity to meet with Him every day. It's natural to wonder what happens to those who never hear about

Jesus, but God graciously reveals Himself to all people through creation (Romans 1:18-20) as well as in unmistakable dreams, visions, and personal encounters (Acts 9:3-5, Matthew 27:19, Revelation 14:6-7). Jesus graciously spares all children from judgement (Matthew 19:14, Deuteronomy 1:39, Job 3:16-17, Revelation 20:11-15), but the fact remains that some people choose to reject the one true God.

Reconciling the existence of hell with a loving God can feel difficult at times, but because He values free will, God grants the desires of those who deny Him—anything else would violate our individuality. We can have full confidence that God is right and gracious in His final judgment against sin. Instead of being preoccupied with our own sense of fairness and bearing responsibility for other people's destiny, we must personalize what God has done for us. Grace has reorientated *our* destiny. God rescuing us from the total, never-ending separation from all goodness highlights the magnificence of His grace. By trusting in the grace of Jesus, sin and hell is completely taken away by the cross of Jesus. Completely.

Once we understand the terrible consequences of our sin, we begin to understand the importance of grace—we deserve judgement, but Christ offers us a full pardon. This truth alone can make a completely sane person jump into a swimming pool fully clothed, amongst other outbursts of joy. Not only does God pardon us, He freely credits Jesus' perfect life to us, making us completely righteous in God's sight. The first generation of Jesus' followers understood grace as the central attitude and mission of Jesus, you see "grace and peace from Jesus" in the introductions to nearly all the New Testament letters. The apostle Peter even says: "May grace and peace be *multiplied* to you" (1 Peter 1:2, italics mine), meaning God gives us this unconditional kindness, through His Son Jesus, over and over again.

IN-YOUR-FACE GRACE

Grace never ignores or excuses sin, but unapologetically confronts it. Jesus graciously corrected Martha, not to shame her, but to bring her self-righteousness into the light that she might be free from it. Like Martha, we easily place expectations on ourselves and others and get uptight when those expectations aren't filled, but grace proactively leads us towards freedom. Not with shallow words, but through authentic relationships, and if necessary, constructive confrontation. Grace powerfully free's us from our own legalistic standards so we can sit back, receive, and multiply Jesus' grace to others.

EVEN MORE GRACE

God expresses His over-the-top grace even further through the provision of the Holy Spirit. Jesus and His followers said much about the person and work of the Spirit. He causes us to be born again spiritually (Titus 3:5). In fact, we cannot become Jesus' followers but by the permanent internal work of the Spirit (Romans 8:9). He gives us counsel and help, convicting us of sin and producing fruitful character (John 14:16; 16:8, Galatians 5:22). He guides us into truth, affirming our identity, and crying out to God on our behalf (John 16:13, Romans 8:15-16). The Spirit's presence within us allows us to sit before Jesus like Mary and receive from Him.

Consistent with the nature of grace, we see abundant generosity when it comes to the Holy Spirit. Jesus famously said "But you will receive *power* when the Holy Spirit has come upon you" (Acts 1:8, italics mine), but we often overlook the fact that He made this promise to people whom the Spirit had already caused to be born again (Matthew 16:16, John 14:17, John 20:22). This particular work of the Spirit empowers Christians as witnesses for God to use in supernatural ways.

The church in Acts experienced the connection between prayer and receiving the power of the Spirit. The disciples had devoted themselves to prayer when they first received the Spirit's power (Acts 1:14, Acts 2:1-4). Then the same group of Christians at another prayer gathering were again "filled" with the Spirit (Acts

4:31). Grace dictates that more of the Holy Spirit is available for all believers "...for he gives the Spirit without measure (John 3:34)", which is often received through prayer. If you are a timid witness for Jesus, and have never seen His miraculous works, you have license to request the Holy Spirit's power.

Peter and John prayed for the Samaritan believers to receive the power of the Holy Spirit (Acts 8:14-15). Cornelius, the centurion, was a devout man of prayer, and as a response to his prayers God sent Peter. The final result of his hunger for God was the pouring out of the Holy Spirit's power (Acts 10:1, 44-48). The apostle Paul received the power of the Spirit when Ananias, a normal believer like you and me, laid hands upon him. This happened after Paul had been in prayer, perhaps praying for as long as three days (Acts 9:11, 17). Some disciples in Ephesus were asked "Did you receive the Holy Spirit when you believed?" (Acts 19:2). After being baptized in water, they received the Spirit's power and burst into supernatural prayers among other things (Acts 19:6, 1 Corinthians 14:2).

HOW THIRSTY ARE YOU?

Prayer is a common characteristic in all these experiences of the Spirit's power. The Holy Spirit responds to prayer and produces prayer. The quantity and repetition of prayer is not important. In some instances those receiving the Holy Spirit were not the ones praying. The deeper issue is an authentic thirst, which naturally leads to asking Jesus for the Holy Spirit. In John 7:37-39 Jesus said "If anyone thirsts, let him come to me and drink...Now this he said about the Spirit". In Luke 11:13 Jesus points out that if we know how to give good gifts to our own kids "...how much more will the heavenly Father give the Holy Spirit to those who ask him!"

Expressing a hunger for God in prayer, having others pray, and laying on hands are normal patterns in the New Testament for receiving the Spirit's power. These kinds of encounters are frequently recorded in church history, and they still happen today. I was a Christian for several years before I heard of receiving power from the Holy Spirit. I remember responding for prayer, I felt waves of energy surging through my body, and a passion welling up inside my heart.

Worshipful words flowed out of my mouth that were not my native tongue. I was being led by the Spirit in supernatural prayer. I became a bolder witness, experienced healings, and other such miracles. Not everyone's experience is identical, but receiving power from Almighty God isn't something you miss or forget. Being filled with the Spirit's power is unforgettable.

An unforgettable life is only possible because Jesus remembers us, freely blesses us, keeps giving to us, and promises to pour out the Holy Spirit's power upon us. He gives us life, sustains us, guides and empowers us—not because we have earned it, but because He has earned it for us. Giving good gifts is at the core of His generous nature.

Grace allows us to encounter Jesus by sitting and receiving, like Mary, and not by serving and pointing fingers, like Martha. To be a true friend of Jesus is to listen to His gracious words, to thirst for the Holy Spirit, and to obey Him. In John 15:14 Jesus said "You are my friends if you do what I command you". In the next chapter we will consider the unforgettable fruit of grace as we learn to do what Jesus commands. Not as obligated servants, but as redeemed and empowered friends of Jesus.

My next steps are to...

- [ ] Determine a time and location to rest in Jesus
- [ ] Identify and eliminate time-wasting distractions
- [ ] Seek prayer for the Holy Spirit's power
- [ ] Read chapter 3

3

STEPBACK

Have this mind among yourselves, which is yours in Christ Jesus, who, though he was in the form of God, did not count equality with God a thing to be grasped, but made himself nothing, taking the form of a servant, being born in the likeness of men. And being found in human form, he humbled himself by becoming obedient to the point of death, even death on a cross. Therefore God has highly exalted him and bestowed on him the name that is above every name, so that at the name of Jesus every knee should bow, in heaven and on earth and under the earth, and every tongue confess that Jesus Christ is Lord, to the glory of God the Father. **- Philippians 2:5-11**

It's hard to purposefully step back and elevate others above ourselves when we feel that we might be forgotten as a result. Serving others does not come naturally; we resist it because it costs us time and resources. Do I really have the time for this? Doesn't it encourage irresponsible behavior if I help irresponsible people? Will all my efforts go to waste? All too often, however, another question lies hidden at the heart of these questions: Is this person worth my valuable time?

This attitude completely misses the point of serving.

DELIBERATE ACTION

Philippians 2:5-11 tells us that Jesus did not demand to be treated like God, but instead took on the attitude of a servant. The God of the Bible exists as a community of three persons, called the Trinity: God the Father, God the Son, and God the Holy Spirit. Jesus is equal in every way to the Father and the Holy Spirit, yet He didn't consider it necessary to be treated like them. He didn't demand service, instead He served people. He had no fear of being forgotten or becoming insignificant.

To be like Christ, we must make a deliberate decision to serve. In Philippians 2, the Apostle Paul says that Jesus "*made* himself nothing, *taking* on the form of a servant" (italics mine). These terms denote action. They require intentional effort in order to happen. It's pointless to think about doing something if we never actually do it. Servanthood must result in real world consideration of others.

The power of serving produces unforgettable outcomes because it allows us to see people and situations from God's perspective instead of ours. If all we ever do is receive from others, we start to believe that everyone else exists to serve us and make us more comfortable. We perceive difficult or needy people as an inconvenience or an obstacle, and become frustrated or even angry with them. When we believe the lie that everyone exists to serve us we become blind to God and all that He is doing around us. If we want to see the bigger picture, we need to step back.

THE ATTITUDE OF JESUS

Jesus shows us that the true nature of serving is to make others more significant than ourselves. Not passively, accidentally, or begrudgingly. "Do nothing from rivalry or conceit, but in humility count others more significant than yourselves" (Philippians 2:3). Serving comes from a place of seeing ourselves and others correctly.

With Jesus, we no longer think of ourselves as better than others, we no longer use others to give ourselves a leg up. Instead of helping others to make ourselves feel important, we help others because we see their needs as more important than our own.

If He wanted to act like us, Jesus could have listed many reasons not to come to Earth: "I am God, I have all the power in the universe, and it's not like I need them. Besides, they've wasted all the chances I gave to them, and even if I do go, they won't really appreciate what my sacrifice means." If Jesus had said: "I deserve to remain in Heaven, and humans deserve to suffer and die," He would have been exactly right.

Instead, Jesus chose to list reasons to come anyway: "I want to show them mercy and grace, I love them, and I alone have the righteousness to satisfy God's laws. I don't want anyone to perish; I want them to live forever with me in joy. They cannot help themselves, but I can give them hope and freedom." Thank God that Jesus thinks this way.

Jesus could have rightfully demanded better treatment than we gave Him, but He didn't. We all have equal value before God, but we must count ourselves lower than others and not demand equal treatment. We are expected to live in such a way that ignores the human standards of fairness and our right to equal treatment. If Jesus stepped down, we can step back.

VALUING OTHERS

It's easy to rattle off reasons not to serve. We all have busy lives, and thinking of giving our precious spare time to help others rarely seems very appealing. If we want to be like Jesus, however, we must act like Jesus and think of reasons why we should serve. If God values people enough to humble Himself to serve, how can you or I value people any less?

If we happen to find ourselves in need, we should willingly receive from the generosity of others. After all, it's rude to reject a gift. But those who selfishly expect a handout, or consider themselves unable to contribute to the aid of others, reveal an especially serious devaluing of people. The heart that lives to be served holds itself in high regard and will happily take without consideration. The person who refuses to serve, refuses to grow.

"Let each of you look not only to his own interests, but also to the interests of others" (Philippians 2:3). This scripture expects us to take care of our own affairs. If we don't take care of ourselves we limit how much we can serve others. If our lives are out of control, debt-ridden, and dysfunctional, we become a burden to the people around us and use up resources that could help others. We should therefore take responsibility for everything in our lives, so that we can use every resource at our disposal to help others come to know God. It's the calling of all Christ's followers (Matthew 28:16-20).

SACRIFICE

Philippians chapter 2 tells us that God exalted Jesus to the most prominent position imaginable, which makes Him the most important person ever. Why? Because He made Himself the lowest of servants, He humbled Himself to thankless service and a gruesome death. Jesus is unforgettable. Though this lesson seems counter-intuitive, it is absolutely critical that we grasp it: we become truly significant by becoming insignificant.

We remember those who gave their lives in service of others. Soldier's names are engraved on a monument and we remember them with ceremonies. We observe a minute of silence to honor their memories. We write articles and books about them, or turn their stories into TV shows and movies. We do this because we consider laying down one's life to be a great act of heroism. We honor their actions with what we all want for ourselves, remembrance. Nevertheless, all the selfless sacrifices of men pale in comparison to what Jesus sacrificed.

When Jesus looks at your life, what parts of it will He value and reward? It's simple. He will value that which resembles His own life. Even though He has credited His perfect life to His followers, He still notices our actions and attitudes. When we use our time, resources, and skills to serve others, we are telling Christ that we have a heart like His. Serving qualified Jesus for unforgettable greatness, it will do no less for us.

MOTIVATION

We must take caution here not to switch the means by which we relate to God from grace to guilt. If a Christian doesn't serve others continuously and with the right attitude, will God punish them? No. Jesus has taken all punishment and absorbed the Father's anger against sin. God loves Jesus' followers as much as He loves Jesus Himself. They are eternally elevated in significance because Jesus forever dealt with their rebellion to God. Christ's followers serve from a motivation of grace, not guilt or fear.

We know God doesn't punish His followers, but He does bring discipline in order to produce maturity. He wants the best for His kids. Muscles only grow if they are torn, which doesn't feel good at the time, but results in greater strength. Often God uses serving to test the heart and increase character and maturity. It's not always easy to serve others, but God has a purpose in it: to make His followers more mature.

If we trust in Christ, He assures our place in eternity, but we multiply our eternal rewards by serving faithfully. Our heavenly Father loves us extravagantly, even though He has given us the greatest gift in Christ, He has promised additional blessings that correlate with our works in life. In Luke 19:12-28, Jesus tells a parable about a rich man who, before going on a long trip, entrusted his resources to his servants. When the master came back, he saw that one of his servants had served him very faithfully. "And he said to him, 'Well done, good servant. Because you have been faithful in a very little, you shall have authority over ten cities'". Christ's followers serve others because we know Jesus purposefully remembers to bless it.

One of the most impacting times of my life was serving a church. I served full-time and without pay for a whole year. This act of serving transformed me. Not only did I make many significant relationships, including meeting my wife, but I was changed because I gave fully to something much bigger than myself. I helped a guy quit his drug habit. I mentored several teenagers. I served in a youth group. I used my creative skills to help the church communicate more effectively. I learned to serve in so many ways. I took a step back and had an unforgettable year.

STOP ACTING LIKE A BABY

Selfishness seems to be hardwired into us. At some point or another, we all got away with selfishness as kids. Growing up self-centered lays a poor foundation for serving each other as adults. The sooner we can all learn to play well with others, the better. The best time to start is now. Let's put the past behind us and not waste another chance to learn how to serve.

If you think of life as a play, each of us has the opportunity to play a part; but only if we remove ourselves from the audience and join the other actors. The practice of serving is like a rehearsal in a play. Instead of feeling content to merely watch things unfold, we can engage the story by playing a part in it. If we participate in a way that hogs the spotlight, we diminish the other parts of the story. Nothing makes sense, everyone is frustrated, and we ruin the play. If we have a proper view of our part, we see the significance of others and step back from the spotlight. The story shines through, everyone enjoys the experience, and the play is a success. We must quickly move from the audience to being a participant.

WHERE TO START

The world's problems can seem overwhelming. How do we respond? We should prayerfully consider each serving opportunity, especially those right in front of us. We could help our family members, friends, co-workers, strangers, the person next door or across the street if we would count the reasons to help them. A life of service becomes a source of joy when it becomes a part of the rhythms in our lives and flows from a heart that trusts in Jesus.

"As each has received a gift, use it to serve one another, as good stewards of God's varied grace" (1 Peter 4:10). The apostle Peter tells us that because we have received gifts from God, we should use them to serve one another. If we want to use our gifts responsibly, we must serve the people in the church. Let's not waste our opportunities to serve God's people in unforgettable ways.

Look for opportunities in your life to serve others. Don't be afraid of investing your time to make a difference in someone's life. Don't shy away from asking the church where you can help. You can start with something simple, like a one-time serving opportunity. Many people faithfully serve the church each week and they would love to be asked if they had an opportunity for you to help out. Check the information that's provided for serving opportunities. Make sure you count the reasons why those people are more significant than you. Step back.

In the next chapter we will explore one of the greatest temptations we face and how so many of us have already succumbed to it.

My next steps are to ...

☐ Ask Jesus to give me a servant's heart
☐ Initiate opportunities to help others
☐ Seek an opportunity to serve the church
☐ Read chapter 4

4

GIVEBACK

[Jesus] sat down opposite the treasury and watched the people putting money into the offering box. Many rich people put in large sums. And a poor widow came and put in two small copper coins, which make a penny. And he called his disciples to him and said to them, "Truly, I say to you, this poor widow has put in more than all those who are contributing to the offering box. For they all contributed out of their abundance, but she out of her poverty has put in everything she had, all she had to live on" - **Mark 12:41-44**

Giving like this has been a normal part of worship for centuries. Unfortunately, some Christians today overlook the offering altogether, but this widow didn't, and neither did Jesus. As we have found out, Christ purposefully remembers what we do, and now this little widow has the privilege of teaching us through the example she set. Though she thought herself and her gift insignificant, Christ has made her significant forever.

With each telling of her story, this widow helps others become more generous; her example multiplies financial resources to the poor and helps people come to know and worship Jesus. Her attitude has impacted people across the globe for 2000 years, and will continue to do so until the end of the world. Never discount the little things we do in life, Jesus will use them and remember them for eternity.

MONEY MATTERS

Jesus notices what people do with their money. Why? What is so important about finances that Jesus would be this intrusive? Aren't people's financial contributions supposed to be anonymous? Doesn't it seem wrong for Jesus to evaluate a person based on how much they give?

Jesus talks about money because our spending reveals our heart. We cannot argue our way out of this one: our checkbook, our bank statements, our receipts show an unmistakable paper trail to our priorities. Jesus said in Luke 12:34 "For where your treasure is, there will your heart be also." Wherever we spend or invest our money, that's what we care about the most. Therefore, to change our affections from the things of this world to the things of God, we must change where we put our money. Money has power, and if we don't want money to enslave us, we must learn to become more generous with it.

The Bible doesn't speak out against people having money, but it clearly states that our possessions will rule us if we let them. "For the love of money is a root of all kinds of evils" (1 Timothy 6:10). Money itself doesn't create problems, but many evils in the world can be traced back to people wanting more money and possessions than they need.

ASSESSMENT

Jesus did not interview the widow or the wealthy people or give them personality tests. He merely looked at their giving and then came to a conclusion about their values. He assessed the attitudes of their hearts, not by counting how much they put in, but by observing how much they kept for themselves. Because the wealthy people in this story kept so much of their money for themselves, it revealed that they valued themselves more than anyone else. The widow gave everything she had because she counted herself as less significant. By doing this, Jesus made her life unforgettable.

Perhaps you want to put this book down right now because money causes you so much stress, but the Bible holds the solution to all our problems with money. It has more to say about money than prayer and faith combined. We cannot avoid facing our attitudes and activity concerning money. Anyone who has inherited money (or debt) will tell you that how we handle money has unforgettable consequences. Downplaying the importance of financial stewardship will only cause pain for ourselves and others in the future.

INDULGENCE

Many of us have endangered our future through sinking ourselves into debt because we have allowed things we don't need to consume us. In unique circumstances like sickness, abandonment, or tragedy, debt can be unavoidable. When these situations happen, we need to have compassion and bring relief to the people affected by them. A lot of debt, however, results from a choice of indulgence and self-importance. If all of Christ's followers could get out of debt, we could eliminate a vast amount of global suffering and fund a number of new Christian ministries. Unfortunately, our love of money holds us back.

"He who loves money will not be satisfied with money, nor he who loves wealth with his income; this also is vanity" (Ecclesiastes 5:11). The ancient king knows the score. Acquiring money won't satisfy us and loving money is pointless.

SAVINGS

Perhaps you are a "saver." You dislike spending and think of frugality as a virtue. There is value in not making emotional decisions about purchases, but many savers don't have a real goal behind their saving. The Bible never instructs us to randomly save up money; saving should have a specific, God-given reason. Otherwise we just hoard money for the illusion of security it gives, thinking that God will bless us because we don't selfishly spend on material objects. By having a certain amount of money in the bank, people feel safe and smart. This is just a different expression of self-importance.

This way of operating robs people who have real needs and causes us to trust in ourselves and not in God. When we pointlessly stockpile money in bank accounts that could alleviate suffering and support faithful Christians who serve God, it's an injustice. In the end, saving without purpose and spending without prudence both show we've fallen into the trap of generosity toward ourselves instead of others.

GENEROSITY

To be Christ-like is to give generously and sacrificially. When we experience some level of loss through giving, we enter into the joy of God. "For God so loved the world, that he *gave* his only Son, that whoever believes in him should not perish but have eternal life" (John 3:16, italics mine). There was nothing more valuable to God than His Son, yet He gave Jesus to us as a sacrifice. God knew that pain would be involved, but the pain resulted in enormous joy. This is the nature of giving, it can be hard to start, but once we see the good that comes from it, it's hard to stop.

Jesus takes note of what everyone gives, wealthy and poor alike. It's easy at times for the wealthy, or those who pretend to have wealth, to seem the most generous. Giving large sums of money in public can lead to a false sense of generosity, and often their contribution barely makes a dent in their wallet. Unlike people who merely want others to think of them as generous, Christ gave sacrificially. On the other hand, those who have less can tend to give a bigger percentage of their income because they know first-hand the difference it will make for others. Their gift may seem smaller and so they might have no desire for others to know about it. Flaunting or hiding what we give reveals that we base our giving on what others think. Instead, we must base our giving on what God thinks.

The world has many worthy causes and charities, but God specifically commissioned the church to serve the spiritually and materially poor. Giving equips the church for that mission. Our giving also shows our gratefulness to God. "For the ministry of this service [giving] is not only supplying the needs of the saints [believers] but is also overflowing in many thanksgivings to God" (2 Corinthians 9:12). In other words, when we invest in God's people, we worship God. Just like serving, we don't lack opportunities to give, only the right heart attitude about ourselves, other people, and where our money comes from.

OWNERSHIP

Our money isn't our money at all.

> Beware lest you say in your heart, 'My power and the might of my hand have gotten me this wealth.' You shall remember the LORD your God, for it is he who gives you power to get wealth. (Deuteronomy 8:17-18)

It's easy to think of ourselves as "self-made." We love to believe the lie that says our money comes from our abilities or education. If our money comes from something that God has given us, however, then even the money we earn or receive doesn't belong to us. Let this truth fill your mind: our ability to make money comes from God; therefore our money comes from and belongs to God.

"The earth is the LORD's and the fullness thereof" (Psalm 24:1). If the earth is God's possession, and everything that fills it, we cannot assume true ownership over anything. Our deeds and bank accounts might have our name on them, but if God owns us, then He owns everything in our lives: our property, bodies, even our ideas.

When we view ourselves as managers of God's money instead of owners, we can freely invest it where He wants, without the fear of our needs being forgotten. If we belong to Christ, God will take care of us.

> Look at the birds of the air: they neither sow nor reap nor gather into barns, and yet your heavenly Father feeds them. Are you not of more value than they? And which of you by being anxious can add a single hour to his span of life? (Matthew 6:26-27)

Jesus assures us that we don't need to be anxious; our Father in heaven values us. If God feeds birds, He'll certainly feed us.

Jesus gives us an enormous incentive to give up earthly things and pursue a relationship with Him. In Matthew 19:29, He not only promises us eternal life, He also assures us that whatever we give up for His sake, we will receive back a hundred fold. We can be excited about living with God and receiving His generous gifts, knowing that anything we give Him will earn us a 10,000% interest rate. Putting our money into God's plans pays off better than the financial investments we make on earth. Plus, none of them offer such an extravagant interest rate. Only a fool would refuse such an offer.

YOUR GIFT

The widow in Mark chapter 12 gave at her local temple in order to express her worship and devotion to God. She invested in the work God was doing through His people. She had to give her money in such a way that Jesus could see exactly what she put in. She had only two coins, but she still gave. As long as you and I have money, we can afford to give. If you can read this, you can get and give money.

Why not take a baby step and test what God says by giving a contribution to the church? It's important to find out how you can give, whether it's online, through an app, with a giving envelope, or in the public offering. Just like that widow gave in such a way that was observable to Jesus, it's important to make your gift observable to those receiving it. If you have the opportunity to provide contact information, go ahead and give it, not to boast, but to make you accountable to any future giving. This contribution might also help reduce your taxes.

If you have suspicions about the motives behind this request, then give your gift elsewhere, but give first to God's plan and purpose. In Matthew 6:25-33, Jesus tells us not to worry about our clothing or food, but instead to "seek first the kingdom of God and his righteousness, and all these things will be added to you." If we seek God first, if we put our money into His kingdom before we put it anywhere else, then He promises to give us all the things we need.

If you want to trust Jesus, you need to trust that He has a plan to provide for you. The worst that can happen is that you have a bit less, and someone else is helped and blessed by having a bit more. If everyone lived this way, it would change the world.

PROVISION

During the year of service I did for my home church, I ran out of money. I had invested everything I had to serve God for that year and I needed some cash. I sat in my room and prayed, and when I looked up, I saw a small envelope sticking out of the top of my backpack. I don't know who put it there, but it contained the money I needed at that moment. My heart overflowed with joy and gratefulness as I began to understand that God will always supply my needs, and sometimes more.

God often uses other people to bless us, which means He can use us to bless other people. Giving to God is a joyful experience, especially if we remember that God knows and provides for our needs. As we prove ourselves faithful and generous with money, God often entrusts us with greater things because He knows we'll handle them correctly. Let's start living an unforgettable life by beginning a journey of generosity.

EXTRAVAGANCE

How much do you want to reap?

The point is this: whoever sows sparingly will also reap sparingly, and whoever sows bountifully will also reap bountifully. Each one must give as he has decided in his heart, not reluctantly or under compulsion, for God loves a cheerful giver. And God is able to make all grace abound to you, so that having all sufficiency in all things at all times, you may abound in every good work. (2 Corinthians 9:6-8)

Learning to handle money wisely takes time and effort, but growing in generosity can start today. The Bible has much to teach us about giving, and there is a wealth of Christian resources about finances if you have specific questions about how to get out of debt or how to invest. Don't hesitate to soak up God's wisdom about money.

Up to this point I have asked you to come back to church, to sit before Jesus, to serve and to give, in other words, to take a few basic steps in following Jesus. I want to see you grow in spiritual maturity in Christ, as you learn to imitate the life of Jesus. I'm asking you to take a few hours of your time to bless others and invest in your own personal growth by doing a few simple things.

In the next chapter, I will address the common pitfalls into which many well-intentioned people stumble. We all know that the pressures of life can take over at any moment. Please continue in the pursuit of an unforgettable life as we learn to fightback.

My next steps are to ...

☐ Pray for a heart of generosity
☐ Seek out Christian financial resources
☐ Give a gift to the church
☐ Read chapter 5

5

FIGHTBACK

But he [Jesus] said to him, "A man once gave a great banquet and invited many. And at the time for the banquet he sent his servant to say to those who had been invited, 'Come, for everything is now ready.' But they all alike began to make excuses. The first said to him, 'I have bought a field, and I must go out and see it. Please have me excused.' And another said, 'I have bought five yoke of oxen, and I go to examine them. Please have me excused.' And another said, 'I have married a wife, and therefore I cannot come.' So the servant came and reported these things to his master. Then the master of the house became angry" - **Luke 14:16-21**

The Bible predicts a celebration meal in heaven (Revelation 19:9). But the parable above doesn't depict something that happens in eternity. When the banquet starts to fill up, the servant goes to find more guests. Those he invites are going about their daily business (one of them has recently married); this party isn't a metaphor for the after-life, it's happening right now. The question is, where?

Here's a clue: in verse 23, God refers to the banquet as a "house." The Apostle Peter says: "you yourselves like living stones are being built up as a spiritual *house*" (1 Peter 2:5, italics mine). God doesn't use bricks and mortar to build His church, He builds His church with people. Among other things, the banquet represents the gathered church. It's a feast with Jesus and His people.

PROVOKING LOVE

Our hectic schedules make it easy for us to reject Jesus' invitation, and so we make excuses. Life comes at us relentlessly, and we allow the situations that pop up every day to take over our schedule. Stress warps our ability to discern what is truly important and makes it easy to overlook the most important thing in life: Jesus and His people.

The master's anger in this parable shows us that God finds our excuses to avoid Him unacceptable and invalid. If everyone we knew made up phony reasons to avoid us, our anger would flare up as well, not out of hatred for them, but out of love. If something separates us from what we want and love, we get angry. God wants to be with us, He loves us, and when we make excuses to avoid Him, He gets angry. If He didn't get angry, it would mean He didn't love us. Our excuses provoke His love for us.

FAULTY THINKING

The stress we experience in our lives comes more from ourselves than our surroundings, and the more we feed our stress with attention, the bigger our problems seem. The bigger our problems seem, the more excuses we tend to make for them. Soon it can feel as though uncontrollable forces push us around, and we have no say in the matter. We feel like we can't take responsibility for our lives because we don't fight back.

We use all kinds of faulty logic to justify our choices and behavior. If we want to stop making excuses, however, we have to shift blame from the external things in our lives, and focus it on our own patterns of thinking. The real issue lies not in our situation, but how we think of our situation. The next time you feel your interest or desire to follow Christ is under attack, don't surrender and make an excuse. Fight back.

Late one Saturday night, my computer died. Though I had a recent backup, the process of waking up early the next day, driving to the computer store, and getting it fixed took a long time. At the end of this lengthy procedure, I felt irritated, as though I had wasted the whole day. Before my computer got fried, I had been looking forward to going to church. Though I actually had the time to do both, my situation seemed so urgent that it kept me from doing what I knew I would enjoy. I surrendered to my situation and made an excuse. I failed to fight back.

EXCUSE NUMBER ONE

Let's take a look at the excuses from Jesus' parable in Luke 14 that keep us from responding to God. The first person made an excuse not to attend because he placed too much value on his possessions. In the Old Testament, God promised the Jews the land of Israel, and they wrapped up a lot of their cultural and religious identity in possessing the "Promised Land."

Some of Jesus' first disciples owned parts of this "promised land," but many of them did something unimaginable; they sold it. The Bible says of the 1st century church:

> There was not a needy person among them, for as many as were owners of lands or houses sold them and brought the proceeds of what was sold and laid it at the apostles' feet, and it was distributed to each as any had need. (Acts 4:34-35)

If that land was given to them by God, why sell it? Because they understood something profound: God's people—the church—matter more than land and homes. God doesn't require all His followers to sell their stuff like this, but if He ever asks you to sell some of your possessions, you will gain much more than you will lose. God is preparing an eternal dwelling place for us. This divine inheritance will far outweigh any land, home, or object we will ever own under the sun.

When we neglect our spiritual home for our physical home, we provoke God. I'm not talking about things popping up now and again that need honest attention; I am talking about us loving perishable things more than imperishable things and making excuses to love God less than we should. Why reject a house that will last forever for a house that will burn?

EXCUSE NUMBER TWO

The next person in the parable made an excuse because he placed too much value on work. God wants us to be responsible with the talents He has given us to provide for ourselves and others, but many of us feel the drive to constantly work, study, or check on our investments. We can't relax. We don't have time to sleep. We can't switch our minds off. Working six days a week doesn't seem to be enough either, so some of us don't bother taking a day off. Jesus considers this to be an invalid excuse.

God never intended our work to replace Him. The fear of losing money, opportunity, or success leads many to elevate work over everything. We have one or two short chances each week to worship, connect, and serve; yet we willingly give up that privilege in order to work. When we work constantly, we don't allow God to provide anything for us, we grow weary, and miss out on amazing blessings.

We have a man in our church with a very demanding job which puts him under a lot of pressure. He works for some very large companies; if he makes mistakes, the consequences are big. Between the constant stress and travel of his job, he has plenty of excuses not to respond to Jesus, but he faithfully shows up at church and plays his part. He places a high priority on responding to Jesus' invitation. He plans his schedule carefully because he values being with Jesus and His people. He makes no excuses. He doesn't surrender to his situation; he fights back.

We've seen people ask for Sundays off or offer to take over scheduling altogether. Not everyone achieves this level of flexibility, but more importantly, they prayerfully submitted it to God and took action. They fought to be with Jesus and His people.

EXCUSE NUMBER THREE

The final bad excuse comes from a man who placed too much value on his family: "I have married a wife, and therefore I cannot come" (Luke 14:20). But the Bible says:

> "Therefore a man shall leave his father and mother and hold fast to his wife, and the two shall become one flesh." This mystery is profound, and I am saying that it refers to Christ and the church. (Ephesians 5:31-32)

The union and exclusive intimacy of a man and woman in marriage exists to reveal the profound love that Christ has for His church. How ironic that we can let our family distract us *from* Jesus when God created it to be an advertisement *for* Jesus.

For us to tell Jesus that we aren't interested in loving His people because our family takes priority just doesn't make sense. Would you rather look at a movie poster for two hours than watch the actual movie itself? Would you say getting a postcard of Paris is better than going to the city of Paris? How then can we replace God's unforgettable family with our earthly family? It's the worst excuse of the bunch.

When our parents, siblings, spouse or children become a habitual excuse to devalue Jesus and His people, we often find ourselves skipping church quite a lot. Constantly choosing weekend trips, sports events, or just isolation labeled as "special family time" over gathering with believers can reveal an unhealthy emotional dependency to our earthly family. We must absolutely find ways to value our earthly relatives, but we can't neglect our eternal family.

Families and friends can provide us with love and support, but they can also bring challenges, stress and interruptions: births, graduations, weddings, reunions, and other occasions, the list goes on and on. While we can never ignore these things, we should not allow these events to derail our ongoing participation in the greater event: gathering with Jesus and His people.

TEMPTATION

Life becomes busy, and things happen. Maybe we want to work all the time. Maybe we want to pursue a relationship with someone who doesn't follow Christ. Maybe we struggle with addictions. When we feel tempted, let's not make excuses, let's fight back.

We cannot afford to ignore the promptings of the Holy Spirit when we face temptation. "God is faithful and will not let you be tempted beyond your ability, but with the temptation he will also provide the way of escape, that you may be able to endure it" (1 Corinthians 10:13).

If we repent, God will forgive us, but we still need each other in order to function properly. If your commitment to Jesus and His people drops, then the next time God's people gather, you have little excuse not to show up. Don't let shame or thoughts of failure hold you back. We will not look down on you; we all need God's grace. We love you and want you to live like Christ. Come back.

CONSIDER OTHERS

"And let us consider how to stir up one another to love and good works, not neglecting to meet together, as is the habit of some" (Hebrews 10:24-25). When we meet together to worship God, we inspire each other to grow in our attitudes and actions. The Bible couldn't be clearer. When we form the harmful habit of not meeting with God and His people, we fall away into idolatry and self-centeredness.

Are you tempted to sit at home and watch TV or catch some sleep? How awfully forgettable. There's nothing wrong with watching some TV, or getting a little extra sleep, especially if you are sick or returning from travel. But, Christians without good reason choosing forgettable activities instead of meeting with Jesus and His people are rejecting their purpose in Christ. Why are Christians forgetting God? I hope you feel the urgency of this. Many of us just have a few hours each week to be with God's people, we should make the most of that time and do all we can to remain steadfast in it.

JOIN A GROUP

If you haven't already, I want you to seriously consider joining a church Small Group. Gathering with a larger public group is valuable, but you can learn and grow so much more when you have a smaller group of people around you who know you. There aren't many better things than being with people who want to imitate Jesus.

We could avoid many of the things that derail us if we regularly met with other believers. This means more than once a week. Our ultimate goal in doing this is to form authentic relationships that transcend events and public meetings. This doesn't happen overnight, it happens when people share life together; and it all starts from a simple connection made in a Small Group. The early Christians often met in each others' homes. Why would we do any different?

Fight back when your circumstances create excuses. Fight the excuses. Fight the lies. Fight the interruptions. Fight isolation. Fighting will make you unforgettable.

My next steps are to ...

☐ Make Jesus and His people a priority
☐ Join a church Small Group
☐ Finish the book ...

6

BRINGBACK

*And the master said to the servant, 'Go out to the highways and
hedges and compel people to come in, that my house may be filled'*
- Luke 14:23

Jesus concludes the parable of the great banquet, which we looked at
in the previous chapter, by showing us that God wants a full house.
Every seat taken, and then some. Our heavenly Father appears to be a
bit of a party animal. Jesus said: "A man gave a banquet and invited
many" (Luke 14:16). He doesn't just love having guests; He loves
having *many* guests. The banquet is the gathered community of Jesus
where we receive our marching orders to extend God's invitation.

No matter how we may feel about having guests in our own
homes, if we know the heart of Jesus, we know that He loves guests
in His home. If we want to live an unforgettable life, we need to love
having guests in Jesus' home as well. That means valuing an
abundance of guests in the church. But it shouldn't stop there. We
must also cultivate a desire to invite people into our lives and our
homes. "Show hospitality to one another without grumbling" (1 Peter

4:9). The reason he tells us not to grumble is simple, we tend to grumble about it.

THREE GROUPS

The master in the parable had taken the time to invite the original group twice. In verse 17 we read, "And at the time for the banquet he sent his servant to say to those who had [already] been invited... ." Their refusal to come represents how religious people tend to respond to Jesus. Sometimes religious baggage or expectations make it difficult to authentically respond to God. The misconceptions that religious people have about God doesn't stop Him from inviting them multiple times into His house, and it shouldn't stop us inviting them more than once either.

When the first guests snub him, the master invites the poor and the handicapped. This isn't an allegory or spiritual illustration. He literally invites people on the low end of the socio-economic scale and people who cannot walk, see, or hear. The poor and the sick usually respond to God's invitation more readily because they have a greater awareness of their need for God.

Once the master sees there is still space, he sends his servant out yet again to go and invite people outside of the city. Jesus is telling us something significant here. While our cities are a focal point of invitation, sometimes we must leave our cities and extend God's invitation to people in far-off places. The news about this great banquet should cover every square inch of the planet. God designed His house so that everyone could fit inside it. There's plenty of room.

This final invitation seems unnatural to us. The recipients may speak other languages and have different customs. The thought of leaving our natural surroundings and investing time and energy to deliver these invitations makes us uncomfortable. This is not a simple request. The religious already understand the concepts and speak the lingo. The poor and handicapped can be reached anywhere. People from other places, however, will take much more time. The work of giving invitations at this stage is not for a beginner.

INVITE THE WORLD

Thank God the servant had already developed the necessary invitation skills. He had already faced rejection from the people with fake excuses. He also has a proven track record with the poor and handicapped. The servant's persistence and faithfulness with the simple invitations in his own city gave the master confidence to send him on a more distant mission. Without that time of learning and testing from the first two groups of people, the servant wouldn't know how to represent the master in other places. As the saying goes, if you can't go across the street, you won't go across the world.

It seems clear by the end of the story that the servant represents the Christian. Jesus gives the church a mission to make disciples of every nation (Matthew 28:19). This means training disciples to extend many invitations where they live, to prepare them for the same work in distant lands. The purpose of the church is to reproduce invitations worldwide. The more people we bring back to God's house, the more people will fill His house with praise.

SPIRITUAL FOOD

In verse 24, the master says that those who reject the invitation will not "taste my banquet." Jesus likens the experience of knowing God to a sensational meal, prepared by God himself. When we bring back others to church, we don't just invite them to a ceremony, we invite people to know the living God and to receive spiritual food from Him. We must never forget that people need Jesus, not man-made religion. We serve them with an invitation so that God can serve them an extravagant meal.

We don't extend this invitation just to get people into heaven, but to invite them into God's purpose right now so they can be fruitful for Him. We are to "taste and see that the Lord is good" (Psalm 34:8). It's important that we invite others to Jesus *and His people*. Everyone needs a context where they can see what God is doing and be fruitful. Without the church these things are nearly impossible. We don't bear the responsibility for how they will respond to this invitation, but we do have the responsibility to extend it. People following Jesus will have different abilities to articulate the invitation. Not everyone will communicate it the same way, but each of us extends it as best we can.

BE COMPELLING

In Luke 14:23, Jesus uses a strong word to describe the way we give our invitations: "compel." This doesn't mean to force, but rather to persuade. We "compel" people by being unforgettably Christ-like. Serving them. Praying for them. Listening to them. We must remember that people are not projects or targets, but human beings whom God loves. God has patience and compassion for us, we must have patience and compassion for others.

The timing and persistence of our invitation can also play a key factor in its effectiveness. Certain points on the calendar, such as the beginning of the year and autumn, as well as Easter and Christmas, lend themselves to easy and natural invitations to join God's gathered community. Not that we should wait until those times to bring back others, but many people would especially consider going to church at those times if someone asked them. If someone turns down your request, don't lose heart. Just because they said "No" to your invitation at the start of the year, doesn't mean they will say "No" at Easter.

NERVOUS?

This talk about invitations can make some of us uncomfortable. We may like having a church that's just the right size for us. If it grows we might feel threatened or forgotten. Or we may become nervous when we talk to people about Jesus, but these reasons are self-centered. Whatever feelings we have about inviting others, as long as the banquet still has room, the master will send us out to invite people in. Jesus will always give His church what we need, so we can extend more invitations, to more types of people, in more places, with total confidence.

I once totally butchered an invitation to a couple who lived in the same apartment building. I was nervous, under-prepared, and inarticulate. I didn't give them the correct information. I had been praying for them, but I didn't think they would come because my invitation was so awkward. I could hardly believe it when they showed up at church, let alone when they joined a Serving Team and a Small Group. Then they started giving. Then they went through membership and indicated their commitment to Christ. All I did was pray and give a bad invitation, and God did the rest.

PLAY YOUR PART

Who can you invite? Think of your family, friends, co-workers, customers, classmates, people on your street, or roommates. We can usually think of at least one person immediately and often more. Make a list of their names and pray for an opportunity to bring them back with you. Can't think of anyone? Then ask God to open doorways for you. Make connections as soon as you can. Remember, the first set of guests made the excuses, but not the servant. We don't have a good excuse not to do this.

Jesus asks us to bring people back as a privilege, not a burden. God places people in each of our lives who we are uniquely gifted to reach. He asks each and every one of us to risk reputation and rejection to let the world know about His banquet. Will you help others become unforgettable? Will you consider them to be more significant than yourself? Who will you bring back?

My next steps are to ...

☐ Show hospitality to others
☐ Invite people back to church
☐ Consider joining the church

BE UNFORGETTABLE

I have been bold in asking you to take some important steps. I believe in people becoming disciples of Jesus, and I don't want to reduce the gospel to merely a way out of hell and into heaven. Of course we know that Jesus prepares a place in heaven for us, but He also has a great purpose for us right now. If we love Jesus, we must also love His body, the church, and His mission to the world through the church.

You may not feel ready to take all of these steps at once. That's OK. Start with chapter one and simply come back to Jesus and His people. You now have a path to follow, just take it one step at a time. I am excited about what is going to happen over the next several weeks and months of your life.

You've already taken the time to come to church. Even if only one thing helped you, hold onto that and thank God for it.

This book asks you to do a few things that *anyone* can do. They don't require any Bible knowledge or any previous church experience. You already have all the necessary tools to do them. If you've already taken the step to come to church, all you have to do next is come back.

If you are free during the next gathering of Jesus and His people, I'd like to invite you back to participate in the unforgettable life God has planned for you.

Remember, come back to Jesus and His people, sit back and receive grace and power, step back and serve others, give back to God, fight back by joining a Small Group and bring people back with you.

Jesus calls you to an unforgettable life, will you accept it?

ABOUT THE AUTHOR

Matt Sweetman is the founding pastor of Trinity Church in Chicago, Illinois. Launched in 2010, Trinity seeks to be a reproducing and disciple-making church. Matt is married to Heather and they have four children, Jones, Macrae, Paisley, and Finley.

UNFORGETTABLENESS.COM

Visit unforgettableness.com to purchase copies of this book.

If you found this book helpful, please consider leaving a review at unforgettableness.com/review

ACKNOWLEDGMENTS

I have received a lot of help with this book. It would not be what it is without the input, skill and support of others. Thanks to all the leaders, speakers and authors who have inspired me.

Special thanks to those who helped with editing: James Priest, Heather Sweetman, Greg Tiffany, and Tim Chambers. I am also indebted to Carl and Virginia Herrington for affording me time and space to write in their house and my brother Dan Sweetman for connecting me with James Priest, who became my primary editor.

Huge thanks to Jesus Christ for saving me and giving me every ounce of my abilities and ideas. I owe you everything.

APPENDIX

HOW TO MAKE FRIENDS AT CHURCH

For churches to become true communities, we must be willing to deal with the difficulties and disappointments of developing meaningful relationships. If we want healthy relationships, we must set healthy expectations of ourselves and others. Here are a few pointers.

BE PATIENT

Connections can happen quickly, but real relationships require time, trust, and effort. Having healthy expectations about how long deep friendships take to build will help us to be patient while we allow God to cultivate our connections into an authentic and fulfilling experience of community. Because of grace, we can enjoy the process while we wait for the end result.

BE A FRIEND

One of the greatest traps in relationships is wanting a friend instead of being a friend. When we expect others to do things for us, hang out with us, and invite us into their lives, we can easily feel excluded. Sometimes other people don't feel connected in the same way, or maybe barriers exist that we don't see. We may be used to giving up on people who don't reciprocate or pay attention to us, but grace enables us to listen, serve, and encourage others with kindness regardless of how our efforts are received.

BE GRATEFUL

Some people will have an easier time making friends than others, which can lead to feelings of resentment and jealousy. Grace allows us to overcome these feelings by celebrating the relationships that others enjoy and also by showing us how our actions and attitudes can affect others, either positively or negatively. We can trust God to give us the relationships we need while we continue to be good friends to others.

BE REALISTIC

Desiring special attention from spiritual leaders is common, but not everyone can cultivate deep relationships with every leader. As with relationships with other people, our expectations of leaders in the church can sometimes be unrealistic and even unhealthy. God uses different contexts, people, and leaders to change and grow us. Embracing this truth will help us pray for our leaders, be a friend *to* them, and seek their counsel when appropriate. Trust that God will put you in the relationships you need.

BE PROACTIVE

If you're unsure where to start, coming to church consistently, introducing yourself, grabbing lunch with someone, joining small groups or serving teams, showing hospitality, and officially joining are all great ways to get to know people. While you make those connections, pray that God will give you boldness, healthy expectations, and fruitful friendships. Pray that He will show you how to be a godly friend and how to trust His timing and plan. Above all else, seek to love Jesus and remember that He has promised to give you everything you need (Matthew 6:33; 7:9-12).